HANDBAG COLLECTION

Regain your **figure** after **childbirth**

• JILL GASKELL •

GW00721995

BOATSWAIN PRESS

EMSWORTH

Introduction

For many women, having a baby is one of the greatest moments of their life. However, as the initial euphoria wears off, it becomes obvious that getting your body back into shape is going to require more than just a high degree of hope.

This book will help you restore your figure by providing expert guidance and a series of safe and effective exercises which are easy and quick to perform. The exercises are preceded by general advice for exercise in the postnatal period, and an insight into the major physiological changes that occurred during pregnancy and how these affect your getting back into shape afterwards. For ease, the baby is referred to as 'him' throughout.

When can I start to exercise?

You can never start too soon and one or two exercises can even be commenced on day one. The sooner you start the better, as these exercises will also enhance the way you feel. Often we all have the greatest of intentions to exercise and regain our figure following pregnancy but soon find the demands of a newborn baby take over. Whilst it is important to capitalise on this desire from the word go, you should also be realistic and not overdo it. Your body needs time to adjust to caring, and possibly feeding, a new born baby. Attempts to do too much too soon will be detrimental to your recovery and could affect your baby.

Follow the schedule suggested in the gentle postnatal programme 'one' for the first 6 weeks and remember that little – and often – is the key to sucess. Some time after this you can, and should, look to increase the amount of exercise you do – the postnatal programme 'two' will provide an effective but gradual progression. Before starting this or any other more comprehensive exercise programme however, you must check with your medical practitioner that it is all right for you to progress. The 6 week postnatal checkup is an ideal opportunity for this.

Following a caesarean section, recovery is a little slower than that of mothers who had a normal delivery. The sequence of exercises outlined in the postnatal programmes are suitable for both but, if you had a caesarean section or a particulary difficult birth, you should take an even more gentle approach.

When is it safe for me to go swimming?

Swimming is an excellent form of exercise for you as it does not place stresses and strains on the joints or pelvic floor. You are however advised to wait until after your 6 week postnatal check-up before returning to swimming, you can go a little earlier providing the discharge has stopped. It is important to be sure your body is sufficiently recovered and there is no risk of infection. Start off gently and build up the speed and distance gradually.

How often can I exercise?

At first you should see exercise as something to be integrated into your day as opposed to embarking on long and comprehensive exercise programmes. Caring for a new born baby can be quite physical in itself and, together with disturbed sleep, places quite strenuous demands on your body. At first being generally active, practising a few specific exercises and taking your baby out for walks will be sufficient. Look to gradually build up the length of your walks over the first 6 weeks, but remember – do not expect to do too much too soon.

The pelvic floor contractions and tummy tighteners prescribed in the postnatal programme 'one' are very gentle but extremely important exercises and should be practised as often as possible throughout the day. The other exercises within this very short programme, which should be practised at least once a day, can also easily be incorporated into daily activities. For example the squat exercise from postnatal programme 'one' can be practised whilst picking your baby up or putting him down.

After 6 weeks, and if you feel you can find the time and the energy to do more exercise, you can try the full exercise programme outlined in the postnatal programme 'two'. You need only do this programme every other day as your muscles need a day's rest between each exercise session to recover. However, the pelvic floor and tummy tighteners should become a part of your daily routine and you should continue to practise them as often as possible for the rest of your life!

When should I exercise in the day?

At first, it is unrealistic to think you can set yourself a regular time to exercise each day when you have to continually answer the demands of a newborn baby. However, after 6 weeks, when you may find your baby is beginning to fit into some sort of routine, aim to set aside some time – roughly the same each day – when you feel your baby will allow you a few minutes to yourself to exercise. It is important for you to find time to do something for yourself. You may feel the best time is when he is having a nap or you may prefer to include him in your exercise session, using it as a sort of play session at the same time. Suggestions are given within the exercises as to how you can exercise with your baby.

If you are breastfeeding it is always a good idea to exercise after a feed, as exercise can cause full breasts to leak.

How do I know I am doing enough?

For exercise to be effective you have to work hard enough to feel the effects of the exercise, nevertheless you should not work so hard as to end up feeling sore and exhausted. Check with the instructions for each exercise as to how much to aim for and what you should feel during each specific exercise.

The exercise programmes outlined in this

book concentrate on toning exercise – exercise that improves the shape, condition and firmness of muscles. The exercises will tire individual muscles more than leave you feeling out of breath. For toning exercise to be effective it has to make the muscles work a little bit more than they are comfortable with. You should therefore exercise a muscle until it aches a little, after a rest you could repeat the exercise until the muscle aches again. If you feel your muscles burning you have done too much. Rest them and move onto the next exercise.

When will I lose weight?

It is never advisable for mothers who are breast feeding to go on a diet although breast feeding is thought to enhance the weight loss process. By following a sensible approach to exercise and diet you will find your weight goes down quite naturally and your figure improves. Look to include plenty of walking into your weekly schedule as this effective form of aerobic exercise will contribute to sensible weight reduction. Mothers often find the last few pounds quite difficult to shift, in this case wait at least three months or until you have finished breastfeeding, then you can look to increase your exercise and perhaps reduce your intake if necessary. A flabby tummy months later is often due to a little excess fat and lack of muscle tone. Exercise and diet combined should solve the problem.

What makes a good exercise session?

Any comprehensive exercise session should start with a warm-up and end with a cool-down. An adequate warm-up consists of mobility exercises to loosen specific joints, some general rhythmic warming exercises to promote the circulation followed by some stretching exercises to promote an increased range of movement and relaxation within the muscles and joints. The body will then be warm and well prepared to work hard and safely in the main exercise session.

An adequate cool-down consists of stretching exercises to promote relaxation and suppleness within the muscles and joints. Since the muscles are warm at the end of the workout, it is an ideal time to stretch. Because of the effect of some hormones, stretches performed postnatally should generally be short and aim to promote relaxation rather than to increase suppleness. The cool-down should leave you feeling refreshed and relaxed, completing an invigorating, but not exhausting, exercise session.

The workout section of an exercise session will include toning or aerobic exercise – longer exercise sessions can include both. Toning exercise targets the muscles and consists of repetitions of a specific movement, curl-ups which work the abdominal muscles are an example of toning exercise. Toning exercise makes a major contribution to a firmer, more shapely, figure. Aerobic exercise works the heart and lungs and consists of rhythmical whole body movements to promote the circulation, raise the pulse and get you huffing and puffing a little. Brisk walking, jogging, cycling and swimming are all excellent aerobic activites. Aerobic exercise is very effective in burning up calories, making a major contribution to any weight loss programme. Aim to incorporate some aerobic activity into your weekly schedule, for example walk at a brisk pace when taking your baby out for a breath of fresh air.

What you should know about the body
The effect of the hormone - Relaxin

In order for your body to accommodate the growing baby and facilitate childbirth, a hormone (relaxin) is released during pregnancy. Relaxin softens the fibrous tissue within the pelvis allowing it to expand slightly. Unfortunately the action of relaxin is not restricted to the pelvis – it affects all fibrous tissue in the body.

Relaxin and the joints

The effect of relaxin results in a slight softening of all the ligaments (the nuts and bolts of the joints) in the body, leading to a reduction in the stability of the joints. This can also lead to increased suppleness, an occurrence often noticed by women during pregnancy. Extra care is necessary when exercising to check that each exercise is performed correctly and carefully. This will ensure no excess stresses and strains are placed upon the joints which could increase the risk of injury. Check that you maintain correct body alignment and that you move with control throughout each exercise. The effect of relaxin gradually subsides following childbirth, but traces can be present for up to 5 months.

Relaxin and the muscles

Muscles are like a piece of elastic, they will stretch quite significantly and then easily return to their resting length. If, however, muscles are over stretched, as in the case of the abdominal muscles during pregnancy and the pelvic floor during childbirth, exercise is necessary to assist them to regain their tone.

The abdominal muscles

During pregnancy the abdominal muscles have to stretch to accommodate an increase in the waist measurement of about 20 inches and lengthen by about 8 inches. To allow for this increase around the waist, they often separate down the midline (above and below the tummy button along the line that can become more pigmented and brown during pregnancy) rather like a zip that splits open. It is important not to overstress these muscles once separation has occurred (in late pregnancy and the early postnatal period) so that it can repair itself satisfactorily afterwards. Postnatally these saggy muscles lack tone and as a result often fail to hold in the tummy to give you a flatter figure or support the spine in a way necessary to protect it from injury. The progression of abdominal exercises given in the exercise programmes will aid the repair of the separation and increase muscle tone. At first you will probably be alarmed at how saggy your tummy feels. Do not despair, practice your tummy exercises regularly – the bath is a great place to start as the buoyancy of the water assists you – and you will soon see progress being made.

Getting up from lying down

Because the abdominal muscles are weak and overstretched, it is important to avoid placing excess stress on them. When getting up from lying down, mothers are therefore advised to roll onto their side and use their arms to push themselves up to sitting rather than performing a straight forward sit up. The reverse applies when lying down.

The pelvic floor

The pelvic floor is a sling of muscles that forms the floor of the pelvis and supports all the contents of the abdomen. Openings from the urethra, vagina and bowel all pass through this muscle layer which has to stretch like the neck of a poloneck jumper as the baby is born. The resulting lack of tone in this muscle often leads to a slight leak of urine on exertion (such as laughing or sneezing). This is a very common problem for mothers and is known as stress incontinence. Frequent practice of the pelvic floor exercise is necessary (and very effective) to avoid the problem persisting. Women should continue this exercise at frequent intervals during the day thoughout their lives, as a well toned pelvic floor not only reduces the problems of stress incontinence, but also leads to an improved sex life. The pelvic floor contraction is detailed in the postnatal exercise programme 'one'.

Are you fit to exercise?

Providing you have not received any adverse instructions from your medical practitioners following childbirth, the postnatal programme 'one' will be totally safe for you to follow.

After approximately 6 weeks – possibly 10 weeks if you had a caesarian – and following your postnatal check-up with your doctor, you can progress to the more demanding exercise programme (postnatal programme 'two') providing you do not answer yes to any of the following questions.

• Do you get pains in your chest or has your doctor ever said you have heart disease, high blood pressure or any other cardiovascular problem?
• Do you suffer from painful or stiff joints which might be aggravated by exercise?
• Are you taking any medication at the moment?
• Do you have any other medical condition which may affect your ability to exercise?

If you have answered 'yes' to one or more questions, consult your doctor prior to embarking on the more comprehensive postnatal exercise programme 'two'.

Safety within the exercise session

• Check you have sufficient space that is free from obstacles in which to exercise.
• Never exercise in socks, bare feet is fine for these programmes.

• Wear a supporting bra and comfortable clothes that allow your body to breathe.

• Do not exercise following a meal, wait at least an hour for the food to be digested.

• Concentrate on the way you do each exercise – remember it is not only what you do, it's the way that you do it.

• If you are breastfeeding, to be comfortable, exercise following a feed.

• The exercise programmes together with the explanations detailed in ths book are totally safe for you and will help you regain your figure quickly and effectively following childbirth. Be careful of following other exercise programmes as they may contain unsuitable exercises for example straight leg raises or straight leg situps.

• Exercise should never be painful, leave you feeling exhausted, or feeling stiff and sore the next day. If an exercise hurts or feels uncomfortable, relax from it then try again, checking your technique thoroughly. If it continues to be uncomfortable miss it out all together or seek further advice from an exercise professional. Many women experience severe discomfort in their pubis symphysis *(front of the pelvis)* during and after pregnancy. Some exercises, especially those that take the feet wide apart or involve twisting, can aggravate this discomfort. If this applies to you, miss out the exercise for a few weeks until you feel the discomfort disappears.

ix) Move with care and control throughout each exercise, never bounce or jerk.

x) Don't expect to be able to do much at first. Be realistic and increase the amount of exercise you do gradually.

The exercise programmes

Before starting any exercise programme it is important that you check your posture. Good posture should be maintained throughout the day. During pregnancy, posture alters to accommodate the weight of the growing baby. Many women develop an increased curve in the lower back which places excess pressure on the lumbar spine. In the postnatal period, poor technique in lifting and carrying your baby plus heavy breasts which can cause you to stoop slightly (leading to round shoulders) can create further problems with posture. As a result it is important to work to regain body alignment and improve your posture at this time.

Cervical region *(upper back and neck)*
Good Posture
Neck extended, back of the head lifted tall, chin in and shoulders back and down.
Bad Posture
Drooping head, hunched and rounded shoulders, chin poking forwards.

Thoracic region *(middle back)*

Good Posture

Ribs lifted, shoulder blades flat at the middle back and back straight, giving more room to breathe. The arms are working hard to support the baby.

Bad Posture

Shoulders rounded so that shoulder blades stick out, back bent forwards and lungs squashed.

Lumbar region *(lower back)*

Good Posture

Tummy flat and lower back lengthened as a result of pelvis being correctly tilted and weight distributed evenly over the legs with buttock muscles tight to stabilize the hips.

Bad Posture

Tummy stuck out and used to support the baby leading to an exaggerated curve *(lordosis)* in lower back; stress on the lower back due to the weight unevenly distributed over the legs.

Postnatal Exercise Programme 'One'

This programme is designed for you to begin as soon as possible following the birth of your baby.

As new exercises are described add them to those already practised on previous days so you build up to performing a series of safe, effective but easy and convenient exercises.

Aim to practice them as often as possible throughout the day – once you have mastered the exercise technique most can be done whilst holding your baby.

Days 1 & 2
1 Pelvic floor contraction
To retone the muscles of the pelvic floor
Sit up comfortably with your knees slightly
apart and your feet flat on the floor. Think of
drawing the pelvic floor muscles up inside,
squeezing around the back, middle and front
passages making sure you take it right to the
front as if to hold back from having a wee.
Hold this for a count of four then let go.
Repeat 5 times an hour!

*Feel that it is the muscles down below working
– Check you are not holding your breath or tensing
any other muscles at the same time – Once you
have mastered the technique you can practise it
standing, sitting or lying*

2 Tummy tighteners

An easy and accessible exercise to practise frequently for the abdominal muscles

Sitting comfortably check that your feet are flat on the floor and your back is up straight. Without holding your breath, try to pull in your tummy so that the waistband of your skirt or trousers feels a little loose. Hold this for a count of 2, then relax. Repeat the exercise as often as possible and aim to increase the length of time you hold it.

Feel your tummy muscles working and aim to be able to hold them in until they ache a little – Check you do not hold your breath or tighten any other muscles at the same time

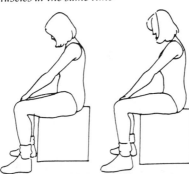

Days 3 & 4
3 Pelvic tilts
To firm up the adominal muscles

Lie on your back with your legs bent and your feet flat on the floor. Pulling in your tummy, tilt your pelvis up towards you so you see it dip in the middle and feel your lower back pressing into the floor. Relax and repeat 4 more times.

Feel your abdominal muscles working – You may find it helps to curl your buttocks slightly off the floor as well (check it's the abdominals working, not your leg muscles) – Ensure you are not holding your breath

4 Alternate heel raises

To promote circulation to the feet and ankles
Standing tall with your feet hip width apart,
raise one heel pressing the ball of the foot into
the ground. Change feet raising the heel of
the other foot off the ground. Increase the
speed of the movement to resemble walking
through the feet on the spot. Continue for
about 1 minute.

*Feel the calf muscles working – Check your posture
and that your hips stay level to reduce the stress
on the pelvis – Keep the weight over the big toe,
press the ball of the foot into the floor*

Days 5 & 6

5 Kneeling hips hitches

To tone the abdominal obliques (the muscles around the waist)

Adopt a position on all fours with your knees directly beneath your hips and your hands directly beneath your shoulders. Keep your abdominals pulled in tightly to keep your back flat. Slowly and with control, sway your bottom from side to side, squeezing your waist muscles and drawing your hip up towards your ribs on one side and then the other. Do this 16 times in total.

Feel the muscles in your waist tighten – Check you do not allow your back to dip – Try to keep your arms straight and your shoulders still

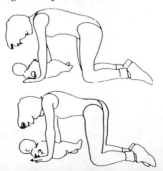

6 Squats
To strengthen the thigh muscles and develop good technique for lifting and carrying

Stand over your baby with your feet apart, one foot facing forwards and the other pointing very slightly out. Bending very slightly forwards at the hips and pulling your tummy in to support your back, bend your knees, checking they follow the line of your feet until your hips are level with your knees. Reach your arms down to your baby and pick him up drawing him in close to you before straightening you legs. Give your muscles a rest before trying this exercise again.

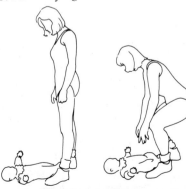

*Feel your thigh muscles working – You may also
feel a slight stretch at the top of your legs around
the inner thighs – Check that your shoulders stay
higher than your hips and your hips stay higher
than your knees – Keep the heel of your front foot
down, the heel of the back foot may rise up slightly
– Tighten your pelvic floor as you pick up the baby
– Think of pushing your knees out as you bend
them so they stay in line with your feet – Hold
baby in close to you supporting his head and keep
your back up straight as you stand up*

Day 7
7 Easy curl-ups
To strengthen the abdominal muscles
Lie on your back, both legs bent, feet flat on
the floor and your head resting on a pillow to
lift it slightly. Place one hand behind your
head for support and the other on your thigh.
Pulling in your abdominals to flatten your
tummy and looking towards your knees, lift
your head slightly off the pillow sliding your
hand a little way up your thigh. Relax and
repeat the exercise up to 4 more times.

*Feel your abdominal muscles working – Rest your
head in your hand for support and to ease the
comfort of your neck – It is a good idea to practice
this exercise whilst in the bath as the buoyancy of
the water assists the curl-up and it is easy to check
that you are doing it correctly – Check your
tummy stays flat throughout the curl-up. If it
bunches up or domes avoid this exercise for a few
more days and continue with the tummy tighteners
and pelvic tilts. The doming is caused by the
weakness of the abdominal muscles and the
separation of the two sides of the long muscle
down the front. You can test for separation by;
placing two fingers crosswise above or below the
naval and pressing them into this centre line then*

raise your head and you will find the two sides
clip/squeeze your fingers if separation is present.

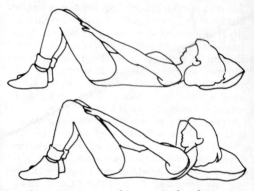

— You can progress this exercise by placing both
hands lightly behind your head and keeping your
elbows out sideways as you curl up

**Continue to practice all these exercises daily
for the next few weeks. As you feel your
abdominal muscles strengthening you can
aim to curl-up a little higher (on condition
that your muscles do not dome) in the easy
curl-up exercise.**

Postnatal Exercise Programme 'Two'

Following your postnatal checkup, aim to follow this 12 minute programme every other day.

Take time at first to learn the exercises correctly then work to establish a rhythm that suits you.

The more effort you put into the exercises the more effective they will be, concentrate on good technique, moving with control and following a full range of movement within each exercise.

Don't forget to practise the pelvic floor exercise. Do 4 before you start.

WARM-UP SECTION

1 Knee bends and alternate arm circles

To promote the circulation and warm you up

Stand with your feet just over shoulder width apart and your toes pointing slightly out. Keeping your heels pressed into the ground, your tummy in tight and your back upright, slowly bend and straighten your legs, at the same time, circling one arm across your body, up over your head and out to the side. Repeat the exercise 7 more times circling alternate arms.

Put lots of effort into the exercise and feel the movement loosening the shoulders – You should begin to feel warm after a few repetitions

Repeat this exercise after each of the following 6 mobility exercises.

2 Shoulder circles

To loosen the shoulders and upper back

Stand with your feet shoulder width apart
and your arms hanging loosely by your sides.
Roll your shoulders in as large a circle as
possible taking them forwards, up, squeezing
them back and dropping them down. Repeat
7 more times.

*Feel the muscles of the chest and top of the back
working and relaxing – Make the movement as
large as possible – Keep your tummy pulled in
tightly to keep your lower back still.*

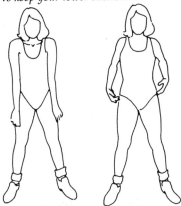

Repeat knee bends and arm circles

3 Reaches

To reduce stiffness in the sides of the body and warm the muscles

Stand with your feet slightly wider than hip width apart and tummy held in tightly to support your back. Extend one arm above your head and reach for the ceiling. Drop the shoulder on the other side. Relax and repeat the exercise 7 more times using alternate arms. *Look up towards your hand and feel a full extension down your side – Do not twist or bend to the side*

Repeat knee bends and arm circles

4 Hip wiggles
To mobilise the lower back

Stand with your feet slightly wider than shoulder width apart, your knees slightly bent and your hands on your hips. Keeping your weight evenly distributed between your feet, tighten your waist muscles and draw your hips up towards your ribs on one side. Relax and repeat to the other side. Repeat the exercise alternating sides until you have done it 8 times on both sides.

Feel your waist muscles working – Aim to keep your knees and shoulders still

Repeat knee bends and arm circles   33

5 Waist twists

To mobilise the spine

Stand with good posture, your feet slightly
wider than shoulder width apart. Keeping
your hips still and facing the front, slowly
twist your head, shoulders and arms round to
one side, reaching round with your arms as
far as possible. Return to the start position
and repeat the exercise alternating sides until
you have done 6 twists in total.

*Feel the movement stretching and working the
muscles in the trunk – Squeeze your buttocks to
help you keep your hips still*

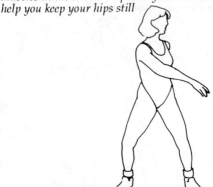

Repeat knee bends and arm circles

6 Ankle circles
To reduce any stiffness in the ankle joints
Standing on one leg rest the toes of the other
foot on the floor slightly to the side. Keeping
your hips still, circle the ankle clockwise,
making the movement as large as possible.
Do 4 full circles then repeat with the other
foot.
*Feel the movement mobilising the ankle joint –
Keep the foot in light contact with the floor*

Repeat knee bends and arm circles

7 Knee lifts

To mobilise the hip joints and promote the circulation

Stand tall with good posture, your feet hip width apart and your arms extended out to the sides at shoulder height. Lifting one knee up towards your chest, bring your arms forwards to end up in front of you at shoulder height. Return to the start position and repeat the exercise using alternate legs until you have done it 16 times in total.

Hold your abdominal muscles in tightly to stabilise your back – Keep the supporting leg straight as you lift the other knee

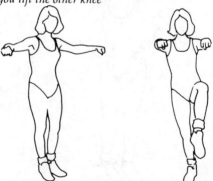

Repeat knee bends and arm circles

8 Shoulder stretch

To relax the muscles of the trunk and shoulders
Stand with good posture, your feet hip width apart and your toes pointing forwards. Clasp your hands together and, keeping your tummy held in tightly, pull in your abdominals and extend your arms above your head. Reach them up and back until you feel the stretch around your shoulders and your middle. Hold for a slow count of 4, relax and repeat.

Check you do not hold your breath – Try to take your arms behind your ears without allowing your back to arch

9 Side stretch

To stretch the muscles around the waist (obliques)

Stand with your feet a little wider than shoulder-width apart, knees bent and one hand resting on one hip for support. Reach up to the ceiling with the other arm. Tilt your pelvis to straighten your lower back then, breathing out, bend sideways, over towards the supporting arm. Reach up and over your head with the extended arm until you feel a stretch down the opposite side of your body. Hold for a slow count of 4, relax and repeat for the other side. Repeat on both sides.

– Don't lean forwards or backwards – Keep your hips centred between your feet

10 Inner thigh stretch

To stretch the muscles along the inner thigh (adductors)

Stand with your feet wide apart and your toes pointing slightly out. Bend one knee, keeping your weight evenly distributed between your feet, slide the other leg away sideways, keeping it straight, until you feel a stretch in your inner thigh. Hold for a slow count of 4, repeat to the other side. Repeat the stretch to both sides.

Keep both hips facing forwards and the feet flat on the floor – If you don't feel a stretch, check your feet are wide enough apart and your weight is evenly distributed between them, bend your supporting leg a little more – If you feel discomfort in the pubis symphysis avoid this exercise for a few weeks

11 Quad stretch

To stretch the muscles along the front of the thigh (quadriceps)

Stand on one leg with knee slightly bent and hold onto a chair for support. Tuck your bottom under and tighten your abdominals to stabilise your back, bring the heel of the other leg back and up towards the buttocks. Hold your ankle and lift your foot to bring the heel in towards your buttocks until you feel a stretch down the front of your thigh. Hold for a slow count of 4, relax and repeat with the other leg. Repeat the stretch for both legs.

Hold the abdominals in tightly to stop the back arching – Keep your thighs parallel (your knees do not have to be together) – If you cannot reach your ankle, loop a towel around it and pull on that

12 Hamstring stretch
To stretch the muscles along the back of the thigh (hamstrings)

Stand with feet hip width apart, one foot slightly in front of the other. Place your hands on the thigh of the back leg for support. Sticking your bottom backwards and pulling your shoulders back to keep your back straight, bend forwards from the hips until you feel a stretch in the back of your front leg. Hold for a slow count of 4, relax and repeat for the other leg. Repeat for both legs.

Check you bend forwards from the hips and keep your back as straight as possible – Do not expect to bend very far

13 Calf stretch

To stretch the muscles around the back of the upper calf (gastrocnemius). Good for cramp

Stand with one foot in front and one foot behind, pointing forwards, hip-width apart. Keep the back leg straight and the heel pressed into the floor, bend your front leg until you feel a stretch in the back of the rear leg just below the knee. Hold for a slow count of 4, change legs and repeat. Repeat the stretch for both calfs.

If you find it difficult to balance, check the feet are not one behind the other – If you feel uncomfortable or cannot feel a stretch, move the back leg back slightly, check it is straight and the heel pressed into the floor

14 Lower calf stretch
To stretch the lower calf muscles (soleus)
Stand in the front and back astride position as for the previous calf stretch. Tightening your abdominals to keep your lower back straight and keeping your heels pressed into the ground, bend your knees until you feel a stretch down the back of the calf towards the ankle. Hold for a slow count of 4, change legs and repeat. Repeat the stretch for both legs.
Check that your feet both face forwards and your knees point in the same direction as your feet – Tighten your buttock muscles to support the hips – If you have trouble balancing, check that your feet are wide enough apart

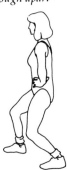

WORKOUT SECTION

1 Armwork

To tone up the muscles in the front and back of the arms (biceps and triceps), reducing flab

Stand with your feet hip width apart and your elbows tucked into your waist. Keeping your elbows tucked in, bend your arms bringing your hands up towards your shoulders. Extend your arms again then, keeping them straight, slowly lift them backwards as far as possible. Repeat the exercise until you have done it 8 times.

For more effect hold something weighing a pound or two – Keep your tummy tight and back still – Try to lift the arms that little bit higher at the back

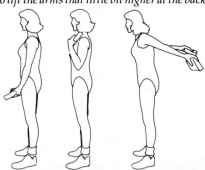

2 Elbow squeezes

To tone the chest muscles (pectorals) and contribute towards a better figure

Stand with your feet hip width apart and your arms out sideways and bent, elbows at shoulder height, fists towards the ceiling. Keeping your arms bent, elbow high and your fist towards the ceiling, bring your arms in aiming to squeeze your elbows together. Return to the start position and repeat until you have done 8in total.

Feel the chest muscles working – Keep your tummy pulled in tightly to stabilise your back – If your breasts are full or sore miss out this exercise

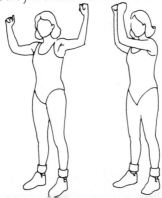

3 Knee bends

To strengthen and tone the muscles along the front of the thigh (quadriceps). Important for many day-to-day tasks as well as appearance
Stand with your feet hip width apart, toes pointing forwards and abdominals pulled in tightly. Leaning very slightly forwards from the hips and keeping your heels on the floor, bend your knees as far as possible without letting your hips drop below your knees. Return to start position. Repeat this exercise until you have done it 8 times.

Feel your thigh muscles working – Check that your knees bend in line with your feet

4 Box pressups

To tone the muscles of the arms and chest

Adopt a position on all fours with your hands directly under your shoulders and your knees directly under your hips. *(Lie your baby on the floor beneath you for this).* Pulling in your abdominals, bend your elbows lowering your face towards your baby. Push up slowly to return to the start position. Aim to do 8.

– Feel the muscles in your chest and arms working – Do not allow your back to dip – Breathe out as you push up – To progress this exercise, lay baby so that his head is a little in front of your hands. Before bending your arms shift your hips and shoulders forwards a little to place slightly more weight on your hands. Keeping the weight forwards bend your arms

5 Kneeling rear leg raises

To tone the buttock muscles (gluteals) leading to a more shapely behind!

Adopt an all fours position as for pressups. Extend one leg out behind keeping your toes lightly in touch with the floor. *(Your baby can lie on the floor between your arms).* Keeping your abdominals tight to stabilise your back and your hips square to the floor, slowly raise the straight leg until it is horizontal to the floor. Relax and repeat 7 times. Change legs and repeat 8 times on the other leg.

Feel your buttock muscles working – Check you do not allow your back to dip or twist

6 Kneeling rear leg curls

To tone the muscles at the back of the thigh (hamstrings) for a more shapely behind!

Adopt a position on all fours, extend one leg out behind you as before. Raise this leg until it is level with your back and horizontal to the floor. Keeping the back flat, hips square to the floor and knee still, bend the leg bringing the heel in towards your buttock. Extend the leg again and repeat 7 times. Change legs and repeat the exercise 8 times for the other leg.

– Feel the muscles at the back of the thigh working
– Concentrate on squeezing the heel in towards the buttocks to make the exercise more effective

ABDOMINAL EXERCISES

Do not attempt to do all of the following 4 exercises the first time you try this programme. Add one new exercise each week over the next four.

1 Curl-ups

To strengthen the abdominal muscles for a flat tum and provide good stability to the lumbar spine

Lie on your back with your knees bent and your feet flat on the floor. You can rest your baby on your thighs or sit him on your hips if you wish. Ensure that you hold on to him tightly with both hands. Pulling in your abdominals to tighten and flatten your tummy, curl your head and shoulders a little way of the floor then lower yourself gently back to the start position. Build up to 8 repetitions in one go.

Feel your abdominal muscles working – Check that your tummy does not dome – Breathe out as you curl up – You can progress by aiming to curl up a little higher, and eventually high enough to give your baby a kiss!

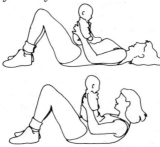

You can also make the exercise harder by sitting the baby higher up your body, as he gets heavier the exercise will get harder!

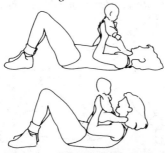

2 Twisting curl-ups

Only progress to this exercise if your abdominals have repaired from separation (see page 27). To provide conditioning for the abdominals with an emphasis on the obliques and contribute towards a flat tum

Lie on your back with knees bent and head gently resting in your fingertips. Keeping your elbows back and your abdominals held in firmly to keep your tummy flat, curl up with a twist bringing one knee in to meet the opposite elbow. Return to the start position and repeat on the other side. Aim to do 8 repetitions in one go.

Feel your abdominals working – Only curl up as far, or as many times, as you can with your tummy staying flat – Check you do not pull on your head with your hands or hold your breath

3 Lying side bends

Only progress to this exercise if your abdominals have repaired from separation (see page 27). To tone the waist muscles (abdominal obliques) and contribute to a flat tum Lie on your back with both knees bent and your feet flat on the ground. Rest your head in your finger tips. Curl your head and shoulders very slightly off the ground then bend to one side reaching round to touch your heel one side with your fingertips. Return to the start position and repeat to the other side. Aim to be able to do 8 repetitions in one go. *Feel your tummy muscles working especially around your waist – Only do as many as you can do correctly with your tummy flat – Breathe out as you reach round to your heel*

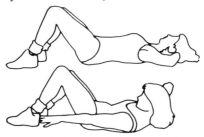

4 Lying side leg raises

To strengthen and tone the muscles of the hips and the outside of the thigh (abductors).
Lie on your side with the underneath leg bent (for balance) the top leg straight (in line with your body) and your head resting in your hand as illustrated. Making sure your hips and tummy face forward and, keeping the hips completely still, slowly raise and lower your straight leg. Do this 8 times.

Feel the muscles down the outside of hip and thigh working – To make the exercise harder, lift your leg as high as you can without twisting the hips

5 Sitting inner thigh squeezes

To tone the inner thigh muscles (adductors), an area that can often become flabby following childbirth

Sit up straight with good posture, on the floor or a chair, and a small cushion between your knees. Breathing out and relaxing all the other muscles in the body, squeeze your knees together and hold for a slow count of 2. Relax. Do this 8 times.

Feel your inner thigh muscles working

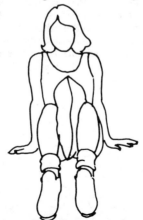

COOLDOWN SECTION

Begin with a pelvic floor contraction.

1 Sitting hamstring stretch

To relax the muscles at the back of the thigh (hamstrings) promoting a feeling of relaxation

Sit on the floor with one leg straight out in front of you and the other leg bent slightly to the side. Pulling in your tummy muscles and, trying to keep your back straight, slowly bend forwards from the hips over the straight leg until you feel a stretch down the back of this leg. Hold the stretch for a slow count of 8 then relax and repeat on the other leg.

If you feel a pull in your back adjust the position of the bent leg – Concentrate on relaxing into the stretch, bending from the hips not the upper back – Do not bounce

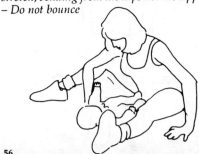

2 Side lying quad stretch

To relax the muscles down the front of the thigh (quadriceps). These muscles can become quite tight and as a result contribute to poor posture

Lie on your side with the underneath leg bent for balance, and your head resting in your hand as illustrated. Keeping your back firm and straight, bend the top leg and clasp your ankle with your spare hand. Gently ease the heel in towards your buttocks and take the knee back until you feel a stretch down the front of the thigh. Hold the stretch for a slow count of 8, relax and repeat on the other leg. *Try to relax in to the stretch – Check your back does not arch*

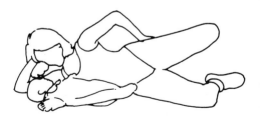

3 Taylor stretch

To stretch the inner thigh muscles (adductors). Releasing tension in these muscles is important to facilitate correct technique when picking baby up off the floor

Sit on the floor with your legs bent, the soles of your feet together and your feet as close to your body as possible. You can rest back on your hands. Allow your knees to flop apart and the weight on your legs to bring about the stretch in the inner thigh. Hold the stretch for a slow count of 8.

Try to relax the muscles, do not bounce or jerk – You can assist the stretch by holding your ankles and gently pressing your knees out with your elbows

4 Sitting buttock stretch

To stretch the buttock muscles (gluteals). Important for good lifting and bending technique

In a sitting position, leaning back on your hands for support, bend one leg placing the foot flat on the floor a little way away from you. Bend your arms slightly to give yourself room between your chest and the thigh of the bent leg. Bend the spare leg resting the ankle, not the foot, across the knee of the other leg. Using your arms, straighten your back and think of folding at the hip joint, move your ribs up towards your thighs until you feel a stretch in the buttocks on one side. Repeat reversing the position of the legs.

Keep the knee of the side being stretched as far away from you as possible – Think of lifting up from the lower back

5 Kneeling shoulder stretch

To stretch the muscles around the shoulder joints

Adopt a kneeling position with your buttocks on your heels, your arms extended in front of you, your hands on the floor, thumbs close together and chest resting on thighs. Keeping your chest low, slide your hands and hips forward, raising your buttocks up off your heels until your hips are directly above your knees. Keeping hips high and arms out straight, push your chest down towards your knees until you feel a stretch in your shoulders. Hold the stretch for a slow count of 8.

Think of a weight pressing down on your shoulder blades – Hold your tummy in firmly to ensure your back does not arch – Check your hips are not in front of, or behind, your knees, you should feel comfortable and balanced

6 Sitting chest stretch

To stretch the chest muscles (pectorals) and relieve any tension caused by heavy breasts
Sit up tall on the floor with your knees bent and your feet flat on the floor. Place your fingertips lightly on the floor behind you. Squeezing your shoulder blades together and thinking of expanding your chest, lift your chest so that it move up towards the ceiling. Look up as well until you feel a stretch across the front. Hold the stretch for a slow count of 4, rest and then repeat.

Rest on your fingertips for support – Don't allow the head to fall backwards

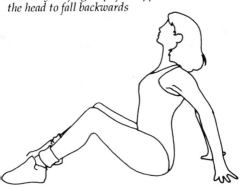

When can I return to exercise classes?

Exercise classes can be safely returned to following your 6 week postnatal check-up with your doctor. Any return however must be gradual and you should not look to start exercising at the level you achieved before your pregnancy. Progress will occur at quite a rate but listen to your body and do not overdo it.

If possible, start with a specific postnatal exercise class for the first few weeks following your 6 week check-up and progress to a beginner class before returning to your more advanced and intense workout. Check your technique carefully to minimise stresses on the lower back or pelvis and only perform abdominal exercises to a degree where you can maintain a flat stomach. If doming occurs the muscles have either become fatigued or the exercise is too demanding. In these instances stop the excercises or seek alternatives.

Exercise classes often include a comprehensive stretch section in the cool-down during which *developmental stretching* is employed to encourage an increase in flexibility. Because of the effect of relaxin, extra care should be taken when performing stretching exercises and women are not encouraged to perform developmental stretching for at least 5 months after childbirth. Keep the stretches short and stretch to promote relaxation rather than stretching to improve flexibility.

Avoid impact work in an aerobics class until you feel your pelvic floor has regained its full tone and elasticity. It is important not to stress an already weakened muscle. If you suffer from stress incontinence, work even harder at your pelvic floor exercises. Impact work also places a high degree of stress on your joints and muscles. Remember, traces of the hormone relaxin can be present for some time and this will affect the ability of your joints to sustain these extra stresses.

Summary

The changes that took place in your body during your pregnancy will affect you for some time following the birth of your baby. Whilst it is not true that you are 'never the same again', recovery should be gradual. Attempts to expect or do too much too soon can lead to problems while the body is still affected by hormones and learning to cope with the added demands of a new baby. It is never too late to start exercise following childbirth but you should always commence very gently and then progress gradually at a rate that is comfortable to you. Understanding the changes that have occurred during pregnancy and how they affect you postnatally will also help. Listen to your body and be confident that this guide will help you regain your figure with ease and interest.

Follow these guidelines to be as safe as posssible in your efforts to regain your figure:–

- *Follow a gentle programme of abdominal muscles exercises. Do not strain them or perform straight leg raises/situps*
- *Practise pelvic floor contractions regularly*
- *Keep a little time each day for the 12 minute toning programme for improved muscle tone*
- *Stand and carry your baby with good posture*
- *Do not diet and exercise excessively*
- *Try some gentle aerobic exericise daily (walking)*
- *If breastfeeding, exercise following a feed*

Above all, remember to listen to your body, take it gradually but be determined to persevere. A little regular exercise will help you to achieve a firm and shapely body.

Best of luck and happy exercising